THE
GOD
KIND OF
FAITH

BILL KINSTON

The God Kind Of Faith
ISBN: 1-59544-531-5

Copyright May 2014
Bill Winston Ministries
P.O. Box 947
Oak Park, IL 60303-0947

Table of Contents

Chapter One: What is Faith? 5

Chapter Two: Enemies of Faith 13

Chapter Three: Where is Your Faith? 19

Chapter Four: God is Looking for Faith 27

Chapter Five: Faith Requires Action 41

⊰ Chapter One ⊱

What is Faith?

The most important thing a believer should know after being born-again and filled with the Holy Ghost is **faith.** It's one of the most important subjects to learn and master in our Christian walk. At least four times in the Scriptures it says, *"The just shall live by faith."* The message here is that faith is a way of living and not a parachute used in case of an emergency. Faith is a lifestyle and not an event. It's how we live, as children of God, every day of our lives.

And to live by faith doesn't mean you quit your job, go on a picnic and feed the birds, expecting God to take care of you. It means that you don't look to the job as your source or supply. You look to God as your source—and to your job or assignment as only one of many channels by which God provides for your needs.

Unfortunately, much of the Church has not been living by faith and has not been taught faith. Consequently, they have been subject to the same hardships as people who don't know God. These hardships are caused mainly by demonic forces and by the curse released into the earth from Adam's and Eve's sin in the Garden of Eden.

So what is faith? Hebrews 11 gives this definition,

> [1]Now faith is the substance of things hoped for, the evidence of things not seen.

Faith is what causes the unseen things (God's promises or truth) to come into visibility to bless you and to bless others.

From the beginning, in the book of Genesis, the Bible tells us that everything was first spiritual before it became physical. All physical things had their origin in the spirit. This physical world is the reflection of the more powerful spiritual world from which it came.

That's why Jesus could release words filled with faith and power and stop a storm. Faith-filled words can bind things and loose things. Jesus said, "My words are spirit and they are life." Words are used to connect the seen and unseen.

Furthermore, spiritual things are more real than physical or natural things. Heaven is more real than the earth. The Creator is more real than His creation. And get this . . . His promises are more real than your problems.

Faith is what I call the *"master key"* of the Kingdom of God. Whether it's prayer or confessions; whether it's using the name of Jesus or pleading the blood; whether it's healing, deliverance, or prosperity; they all manifest when we operate by faith. Even though these things are legally ours and have been passed on as a part of our inheritance when we accepted Jesus as our Lord and Savior, they can only be received by faith. In fact, God does nothing apart from faith.

God is a Faith God...

And He demands faith of us. Without faith we cannot get our prayers answered, and without faith we cannot please God. Hebrews 11:6 says,

> [6]But without faith *it is* impossible to please *him:* for he that cometh to God must believe *that* he is, and that he is a rewarder of them that diligently seek him.

The apostle Paul writes a lot about faith throughout the New Testament:

- We walk by faith
  (2 Corinthians 5:7)

- We take up the shield of faith
  (Ephesians 6:16)

- We fight the good fight of faith
  (1 Timothy 6:12)

- We hold fast to the profession of our faith (Hebrews 10:23)

What am I saying? Simply, as I mentioned earlier, that God demands faith of us. Faith commits God to get involved in our circumstances to bring us victory. I heard a preacher make a powerful statement about faith. He said, "Faith is your greatest (spiritual) asset." Why? Because you cannot even reach your God-given destiny without it. Faith is the holder of your destiny. And in these last days it is the safest place to live.

Faith unlocks a world of unlimited possibilities and connects you to the realm of the supernatural. I have often made the statement that, "The Lord will pass over a million people just to get to someone who has faith." When Jesus stood up in the synagogue and announced His ministry, He said "But I tell you of a truth, many widows were in Israel in the days of Elias, when the heaven was shut up three years and six months, when great famine was throughout all the land; but unto none of them was Elias sent, save unto Sarepta, *a city* of Sidon, unto a woman *that was* a widow" (Luke 4:25-26). What was the affiliation of the prophet to this woman? Her faith.

As you read this book and meditate the scriptures, I pray that God will give you a greater revelation and understanding about the importance of faith, and why God cannot prosper you, protect you, or even promote you apart from faith, whether yours or someone else's.

When you begin operating in faith you become anger-proof, failure-proof and undefeatable. In other words, you cannot be defeated by the adversary or life's adversity. The scriptures tell us in 1 John 5:4,

> ⁴For whatsoever is born of God overcometh the world: and this is the victory that overcometh the world, *even* our faith.

Faith not only gives you the strength to

endure hard times and persecution, but it also empowers you to accomplish God's divine agenda. The apostle Paul writes about Jesus in Hebrews 12:2,

> ²for the joy that was set before him endured the cross, despising the shame.

Like Jesus, every one of us must use our faith to complete our God-given assignment and to reach our destiny. Again, this verse shows us that faith will give you endurance in hard times and keep you in a place of no shame.

God is looking for faith…so let this book help to ensure that He finds it at your house!

Chapter Two

Enemies of Faith

The Bible tells us that every born-again believer has been given **"the measure of faith"** (Romans 12:3). Notice, it didn't say "a measure," but "the measure"…meaning that we all are given the same amount when we are born again.

This faith is referred to as the *"God kind of faith."* Jesus told His disciples in Mark's Gospel, **"Have faith in God,"** or we could say it like this, "Have or receive God's faith." This is the same faith that God Almighty used to create the universe. One prophet of God describes God's faith as *real faith.*

When we use His faith, this "real faith," to understand and to do things that were before impossible, we are now operating in the "class of God," mankind's original mode of operation.

After Jesus stopped a storm in Mark, chapter 4, the disciples feared exceedingly and said one to another, **"what manner of man is this"** (verse 41). It's the manner of man the world is waiting for. Romans 8:19 says,

> ¹⁹For the earnest expectation of the creature waiteth for the manifestation of the sons of God.

Enemies of Faith

Two enemies of this God kind of faith are "sense knowledge faith" and "mental assent." Unfortunately, these two types of faith have been most prevalent in the local church. Let me briefly describe them.

- **Sense knowledge faith** says, "When I see it with my natural eyes or when I feel it, then I will believe." It's the kind of faith that's built on some natural experience rather than solely on the Word of God.

It's the kind of faith Thomas had when he

said in John 20:25,

> ²⁵Except I shall see in his hands the print of the nails, and put my finger into the print of the nails, and thrust my hand into his side, I will not believe.

- **Mental assent** agrees with the Bible, that it came from God, and that every Word is true. But when the crisis comes, it does not work. Why? Because the Word never entered into the person's heart (Romans 10:8).

I heard one Bishop say this…"If your faith has no proof it's a fake." How many of God's people are looking for a church or ministry where they don't have to use "one ounce" of faith. Let me warn you…that's one of the most dangerous places a believer can be.

Other enemies of faith are fear, doubt, and unbelief. They are all designed to rob you of your faith and leave you vulnerable to the devil's assaults.

Job said "For the thing which I greatly feared is come upon me..." (Job 3:25). The Word of God tells us to "fear not"...God "has not given us the spirit of fear, but of power and of love and of a sound mind" (2 Timothy 1:7, *NKJV*). Job returned to faith and God restored to him twice as much of what he had before. He got double for his trouble.

Real faith, or the God kind of faith, says "If God says it's true, it is true." It needs no physical evidence that would satisfy the senses...it acts on the Word of God independent of sense evidence. This faith is much like Abraham had when God told him that he and his barren wife Sarah were going to have a child. "He considered not his own body now dead, when he was about an hundred years old, neither yet the deadness of Sarah's womb" (Romans 4:19).

Real faith is built on the Word of God alone.

If He says "I'm strong"

… I'm strong.
If He says "I'm healed"
… I'm healed.
If he says "He supplies my
every need" … *He will!*

Truth is the highest form of reality. God's Word is **truth**…and **faith** converts things that are **true,** which cannot be seen, into things that can be seen (the physical). Whether prosperity, healing, deliverance, victory, peace…whatever is promised to you by God in His Word…is available and delivered <u>only</u> by faith.

Chapter Three

Where is Your Faith?

"For I say, through the grace given unto me, to every man that is among you, not to think of *himself* more highly than he ought to think; but to think soberly, according as God hath dealt to every man the measure of faith" (Romans 12:3).

This says that every born-again believer has been given the "same measure of faith." You and I were given the same amounts. The difference is whether this measure is being used and developed.

There was a man in the book of Acts, chapter fourteen, who the Scriptures say "never had walked: the same heard Paul speak...and (Paul) perceiving that he had faith to be healed, said with a loud voice, Stand upright on thy feet. And he leaped and walked" (verses 8-10).

Notice, the man had faith, but he was sitting on it, probably waiting on a feeling. Faith is not a feeling, faith is not a product of reason or human logic. Faith is a spiritual force coming out of your spirit (inner man) and once released, will do the impossible. Faith is released the moment we act on the spoken Word.

There was a woman in the Gospel of Mark, chapter five, who had been to many physicians, but continued to "grow worse." The doctors reasoned that she was sick and their human logic had no cure to stop the flow of blood. Understand, I'm not knocking doctors. The medical doctor could be "man's best friend" if that person does not know how to use his or her faith.

Personally, I'm convinced that without the physician most of the Christians would have died. Why? Because they didn't know they had the measure of faith or they didn't know how to use their faith. The difference is that doctors mostly treat the disease, but faith goes to the root of the problem and deals with the enemy who causes the disease. The woman touched Jesus's garment and virtue (divine power) flowed out of Him. He said to her, "Daughter, thy faith has made you whole."

You might be in a place where sickness or disease has had its grip on your body for a time and the medical treatment has not provided any significant relief. Here's the good news, Jesus is the same yesterday, today, and forever. And what He'll do for one, He will do for all. Someone might say "But Jesus isn't here today." Yes, but the Bible tells us…"He sent his word, and healed them, and delivered *them* from their destructions" (Psalm 107:20).

Inside God's Word lies God's power, therefore, when you receive the Word, the power comes on your life to make possible man's impossibilities. When you receive the Word, you also receive the anointing…God's burden-removing, yoke-destroying power. The Bible says in John 1:1, "In the beginning was the Word, and the Word was with God, and the Word was God." What happened to this woman or this lame man the Holy Spirit can make it happen to you...if you believe. Remember, the more you hear the Word, the more faith comes to receive the benefits of the Word.

The Bible says faith comes by "hearing and hearing by the word of God," (Romans 10:17). So the more we hear the Word of God about a given situation...such as "with his stripes we are healed" (Isaiah 53:5) or "My God shall supply all your need according to his riches in glory by Christ Jesus" (Philippians 4:19)... the more faith grows in our spirit about that situation.

From Faith to Faith

As mentioned earlier, every born-again believer has been given **"the measure of faith"** (Romans 12:3). You and I have been given the measure of the God kind of faith, and it is our responsibility to grow the measure that we have been given.

The apostle Paul writes in 2 Thessalonians, chapter 1,

> ³We are bound to thank God always for you, brethren, as it is meet, because that *your faith* groweth exceedingly.

Faith is not designed to stagnate, but to grow, <u>which is our responsibility.</u> Real faith is designed for the impossible, and it should grow to enable you to do bigger and better things for the Kingdom.

In Romans 1:16 Paul said "I am not ashamed of the gospel of Christ..." because the demands of the gospel are things you could be ashamed of that can make you appear not rational. But the things of God are not meant to make sense they are meant to make faith, such as the time the children of Israel marched around Jericho causing the walls to supernaturally fall down or when Mary conceived a child (Jesus) having never known a man. The gospel is often not reasonable to the natural mind.

So, each time you hear and act on the Word of God, your faith gets stronger and stronger, and eventually you can do and believe for things that are totally impossible and unbelievable for the natural man. I like to say it this way, "People of faith should have no respect for the word *'impossible.'"*

That's why Jesus tells us in Mark 11,

> [23]For verily I say unto you, … **whosoever** shall say unto this mountain, Be thou removed, and be thou cast into the sea; and shall not doubt in his heart, but shall believe that those things which he saith shall come to pass; he shall have whatsoever he saith.

This verse tell us that faith will work for anyone (any believer or "whosoever") and for anything (any "whatsoever"), and that **real faith** speaks.

I recall some years back when Chicago had one of those winters with record-breaking cold temperatures, that my car wouldn't start. It was parked out on the lakefront along with other cars that wouldn't start either. I was determined to use my faith. I said, speaking directly to the car... "In the name of Jesus, start!" I went inside the apartment building where I was living to warm up and give God a chance to work. After about one-half hour I returned to the car and turned the key in the ignition. That car started up like it was a normal spring day. Notice, I didn't pray to God about it. I used my authority and spoke to it and the car obeyed me, or shall I say, my faith. God gave us the measure of faith, the same faith He used in creation to do the impossible. In fact, we are created to have an appetite for the impossible.

The human kind of faith is different from the God kind of faith. The human kind of faith says this, "I sure hope I can get my healing" or "God will heal me when He gets good and ready" or "Lord heal me, if it be thy will." Notice the uncertainty. Real faith begins where the will of God is known. The Word of

God is the will of God.

Verse 24 goes on to say,

> ²⁴Therefore I say unto you, What things soever ye desire, when ye pray, believe that ye receive *them,* and ye shall have *them.*

The God kind of faith touches things that cannot be seen or are invisible. Jesus didn't say...feel that you receive them. He said only "believe." This means that if you only operate in the physical, you'll never get what belongs to you. Real faith believes and receives what has been already given to us in Jesus.

Chapter Four

God is Looking for Faith

Luke 18:8 says,

⁸I tell you that he will avenge them speedily. Nevertheless when the Son of man cometh, shall he find faith on the earth?

Remember the four men in Mark, chapter two, who could not come in by the door where Jesus was preaching the Word, so they tore open the roof to let down their friend who was bedfast, sick of the palsy. The scripture reads... "<u>When Jesus saw their faith</u>, he said unto the sick of the palsy, Son, thy sins be forgiven thee." And the man was healed.

Remember the woman with the issue of blood in Mark 5:27-34 who pressed her way through the crowd and touched the hem of

Jesus's robe? She wasn't the least bit timid. She was walking by faith. "And straightway the fountain of her blood was dried up; and she felt in *her* body that she was healed of that plague." Notice how she boldly made her way through that crowd. "And he said unto her, Daughter, thy faith hath made thee whole; go in peace, and be whole of thy plague."

God is also looking for faith today! He is looking for people who will believe Him and receive what Jesus died to provide...the healing, delivering, saving, and protecting power promised in His Word.

Because like the men who broke open the roof to get their friend healed or the woman who fought through the crowd to get healing—you must be bold and believing, never allowing circumstances or how things look to short circuit your faith in God or the power of His promised Word.

Unashamed Faith

God is looking for the kind of faith that

made Jesus stop to heal blind Bartimaeus who cried out in Mark 10:46-52 *(NKJV)*, even when the crowd told the blind man to shut up. I call it, "unashamed faith."

> ⁴⁶Now they came to Jericho. As He went out of Jericho with His disciples and a great multitude, blind Bartimaeus, the son of Timaeus, sat by the road begging.

> ⁴⁷And when he heard that it was Jesus of Nazareth, he began to cry out and say, "Jesus, Son of David, have mercy on me!"

> ⁴⁸Then many warned him to be quiet; but he cried out all the more, "Son of David, have mercy on me!"

> ⁴⁹So Jesus stood still and commanded him to be called. Then they called the blind man, saying to him, "Be of good cheer. Rise, He is calling you."

⁵⁰And throwing aside his garment, he rose and came to Jesus.

⁵¹So Jesus answered and said to him, "What do you want Me to do for you?" The blind man said to Him, "Rabboni, that I may receive my sight."

⁵²Then Jesus said to him, "Go your way; your faith has made you well." And immediately he received his sight and followed Jesus on the road.

I recall the story of how a well known man of God began to preach faith and the message of prosperity. When he started preaching it, he would drive up to the church in an old car that had been wrecked on both sides by his daughters. Some folks didn't quite understand how he could drive that old beat-up car and preach the word of faith and prosperity as he was doing. Well the answer is simple... he had "unashamed faith." He wasn't moved by what he saw in his present condition. He was only moved by what he believed which is what God said. Shortly thereafter, he received a brand new Lincoln Town Car debt-free, exactly what he was believing for.

Unshakable Faith

God is looking for the kind of faith that the religious leader Jairus had when he had run out of options and went seeking a miracle to heal his daughter. The story is given in Mark 5:22-42,

> ²²And, behold, there cometh one of the rulers of the synagogue, Jairus by name; and when he saw him, he fell at his feet,

> ²³And besought him greatly, saying, My little daughter lieth at the point of death: *I pray thee,* come and lay thy

hands on her, that she may be healed; and she shall live.

²⁴And *Jesus* went with him;…

³⁵…there came from the ruler of the synagogue's *house certain* which said, Thy daughter is dead: why troublest thou the Master any further?

³⁶As soon as Jesus heard the word that was spoken, he saith unto the ruler of the synagogue, Be not afraid, only believe….

³⁸And he cometh to the house of the ruler of the synagogue, and seeth the tumult, and them that wept and wailed greatly.

³⁹And when he was come in, he saith unto them, Why make ye this ado, and weep? the damsel is not dead, but sleepeth.

⁴¹And he took the damsel by the hand, and said unto her, Talitha cumi; which is, being interpreted, Damsel, I say unto thee, arise.

⁴²And straightway the damsel arose, and walked; for she was *of the age* of twelve years. And they were astonished with a great astonishment.

Rhema Faith

One of the greatest blessings of being born again is that we now have access to the deep things of God. We move out of the realm of only information and head knowledge and into the realm of revelation.

As I mentioned earlier, faith comes by hearing and hearing by the Word of God, not by praying or fasting (although these are important spiritual disciplines). And there is a difference between the *logos* Word and the *rhema* Word of God. *Logos* means the written word that is understood by reasoning or mental faculty. *Rhema* means the spoken word that is revealed by the Holy Spirit to your spirit and spiritually understood; it comes with "light."

Only what you see becomes yours, because whatever you see you automatically believe and become. This is why one man of God said that "revelation is the greatest asset in the school of faith." You can't see (with your spiritual eyes) and doubt it.

That is why the Psalmist wrote, "Open thou mine eyes, that I may behold wondrous things out of thy law" (Psalm 119:18). Luke 24:45 says, "Then opened he (Jesus) their understanding, that they might understand the scriptures."

The story of Simon Peter and Jesus in Luke 5 is an example of both the *logos* and *rhema*. When Jesus taught the people, He was teaching the *logos:*

> ¹And it came to pass, that, as the people pressed upon him to hear the word of God, he stood by the lake of Gennesaret,

²And saw two ships standing by the lake: but the fishermen were gone out of them, and were washing *their* nets.

³And he entered into one of the ships, which was Simon's, and prayed him that he would thrust out a little from the land. And he sat down, and taught the people out of the ship.

However, in verses 4 and 5 Simon Peter responds to Jesus with *rhema* Word faith:

⁴Now when he had left speaking, he said unto Simon, Launch out into the deep, and let down your nets for a draught.

⁵And Simon answering said unto him, Master, we have toiled all the night, and have taken nothing: nevertheless at thy **word** I will let down the net (emphasis mine).

The result: Peter caught a boat-sinking load of fish!

Faith that Perseveres

God is looking for the kind of faith that caused Jesus to bypass all the sick people at the pool of Bethesda and get to the man who had been there for thirty-eight years waiting for his healing. Let's read John 5:2-9,

> ²Now there is at Jerusalem by the sheep *market* a pool, which is called in the Hebrew tongue Bethesda, having five porches.

> ³In these lay a great multitude of impotent folk, of blind, halt, withered, waiting for the moving of the water.

> ⁴For an angel went down at a certain season into the pool, and troubled the water: whosoever then first after the

troubling of the water stepped in was made whole of whatsoever disease he had.

⁵And a certain man was there, which had an infirmity thirty and eight years.

⁶When Jesus saw him lie, and knew that he had been now a long time *in that case,* he saith unto him, Wilt thou be made whole?

⁷The impotent man answered him, Sir, I have no man, when the water is troubled, to put me into the pool: but while I am coming, another steppeth down before me.

⁸Jesus saith unto him, Rise, take up thy bed, and walk.

⁹And immediately the man was made whole, and took up his bed, and walked.

Seed-Time and Harvest Faith

Again, God is looking for faith in every believer. Whenever God has increased my ministry, He required me to use my faith to do it.

In the earlier years of our ministry in Chicago we used to hold our services in a banquet hall. One Sunday after our last service, I came out of the front door of the facility and looked across the street at a large, almost vacant shopping mall that had been in decline for several years.

As I looked at it, the Lord spoke to my heart and said, "Buy that mall." At that time it was not officially for sale, and had passed through the hands of two owners who were unsuccessful in turning it around. The mall was huge…much larger than anything I could see myself believing for.

You see, the enemy, satan, has cleverly programmed God's people to desire leftovers and little things rather than something big, lavish, and excellent. But once I decided to obey God, He gave me a "seed." Luke 8:11 says, **"The seed is the word of God."**

The scripture (seed) God gave me was in Joshua, chapter one:

> 3Every place that the sole of your foot shall tread upon, that have I given unto you.

Once I began meditating this, the light (revelation) came. My capacity to receive was immediately expanded, and the understanding came of how to do what God was asking me to do.

Then the Lord spoke to my heart for our ministry to sow a financial seed, and when I did, miracles began to happen. We had favor with the sellers and they dropped the asking price down to something unheard of. We ended up purchasing the property for millions less than initially proposed. I'm almost tempted to say, and I mean this in a good way, "We got it at a steal."

Since then our ministry has expanded to

thousands of members; we've won thousands of souls; and the mall and its retail tenants have created some 400 jobs. That's the Kingdom and what can happen when you use your faith to step out on what God tells you to do.

Chapter Five

Faith Requires Action

Remember, real faith always works! "But Jesus turned him about, and when he saw her, he said, Daughter, be of good comfort; thy faith hath made thee whole. And the woman was made whole from that hour" (Matthew 9:22). Faith is a spiritual force, and as mentioned earlier, "the substance of things hoped for and the evidence of things not seen" (Hebrews 11:1).

Real faith will drive whatever is not of God right out of your life. This is the same faith God released to create the world. Once it's released out of the heart of the believer (you), it goes to work making good whatever God has promised. Guaranteed!

Here are some simple steps according to Mark 4:26-29 to develop and operate in the *real* or *God kind of faith.* Remember, consistency is the key.

1. Determine what you want. God gives us the desires of our heart.

2. Identify the scriptures (promises) from the Bible that speak directly to your situation.

3. Begin to call what you want. Meditate God's promises. By doing this you are establishing in your heart the things God has promised. Make sure you say it like God said it. Romans 10:10 says, "For with the heart man believeth unto righteousness; and with the mouth confession is made unto salvation."

4. Become fully persuaded like Abraham who believed "what he (God) had promised, he was able also to perform" (Romans 4:21).

5. Act on the Word of God which releases the force of faith and you will supernaturally have what you say.

Remember, faith sees what hasn't been manifested. It deals with what exists but is invisible. The minute you manifest something it no longer requires faith. Faith is believing, conceiving and releasing (or speaking) until you manifest your desire.

Prayer of Salvation

If you're reading this and you don't know God, I invite you to pray in faith this prayer of salvation.

Heavenly Father, I come to You in the name of Your Son, Jesus Christ. You said in Your Word that whosoever shall call upon the name of the Lord shall be saved (Romans 10:13). I am calling on Jesus right now.

I believe that Jesus died on the cross for my sins, that He was raised from the dead on the third day.

Lord Jesus, I am asking You now, come into my heart. Take control of my life and help me be what You want me to be. I repent of my sins and surrender myself totally and completely to You.

I accept You and confess You as my Lord and Savior. Thank You for making me a new person and forgiving me of my sins. In Jesus's Name, Amen.

(Remember to get water baptized as soon as possible according to Acts 16:33.)

Prayer for Baptism of the Holy Spirit

My Heavenly Father, I am Your child, for I believe in my heart that Jesus has been raised from the dead and I have confessed Him as my Lord. Jesus said, "How much more shall your heavenly Father give the Holy Spirit to those who ask Him." I ask You now in the Name of Jesus to fill me with the Holy Spirit.

I step into the fullness and power that I desire in the Name of Jesus. I confess that I am a Spirit-filled Christian. As I yield my vocal organs, I expect to speak in tongues as the Spirit gives me utterance in the Name of Jesus. Praise the Lord! Amen.

Scripture References:

John 14:16-17

Acts 19:2, 5-6

Luke 11:13

1 Corinthians 14:2-15

Acts 1:8

1 Corinthians 14:18,27

Acts 2:4

Ephesians 6:18

Acts 2:32-33, 39

Jude 1:20

Acts 8:12-17

Acts 10:44-46

William (Bill) Samuel Winston

Bill Winston is the visionary founder and pastor of Living Word Christian Center, a 20,000 member church located in Forest Park, Illinois, and Tuskegee Christian Center in Tuskegee, Alabama. Other entities under his leadership include: the nationally accredited Joseph Business School in Forest Park, with eleven other partnership locations across the United States and internationally; Living Word School of Ministry and Missions; the Forest Park Plaza (a 33-acre shopping mall) and Washington Plaza (in Tuskegee); and Golden Eagle Aviation among others.

He's the founder of Bill Winston Ministries (a ministry outreach that shares the Gospel through television, radio, and other media), and president and founder of Faith Ministries Alliance (FMA), an alliance of more than 540 churches and ministries under the covering of

Dr. Winston in the United States and overseas.

Before starting a business career and later a full-time ministry, Bill served six years as a fighter pilot in the United States Air Force, receiving numerous awards, including The Distinguished Flying Cross, The Air Medal for performance in combat and the Squadron Top Gun Award. He received an Honorary Doctorate of Humane Letters from Friends International Christian University.

Bill is married to Veronica and is the father of three children Melody, Allegra, and David and grandfather of eight.

If you enjoyed this book, here are some related books by Bill Winston that can be ordered at www.billwinston.org.

- Transform Your Thinking
- The Kingdom of God In You
- The Law of Confession
- Supernatural Wealth Transfer
- Tapping The Wisdom of God
- Divine Favor - A Gift From God, Expanded Edition

Connect With Us!

Select teachings are now available in iTunes®

www.iTunes.com/billwinston

www.facebook.com/billwinstonministries

www.twitter.com/billwinstonmin

www.youtube.com/drbillwinston

www.pinterest.com/billwinstonmin

www.instagram.com/billwinstonmin

Phone: 800-711-9327

Let Us Partner With You

Bill Winston Ministries (BWM) is an outreach ministry that shares the Good News of the Gospel through a variety of outlets. From our radio and television broadcasts, The Believers' Walk of Faith program, to our monthly partner letters, crusades, and our website, we are reaching multitudes for Jesus Christ.

Our mission at Bill Winston Ministries is to preach the Gospel of the Kingdom throughout the world, and train Believers how to live independent of this world's system and have dominion over it.

For more information on partnership please call 800-711-9327 or visit us at www.billwinston.org.

Together, We Can Make A Difference!

Prayer, Provision and Power